Searchlight
BOOKS™

How Does
Government
Work?

Judges
and
Courts

A Look at the Judicial Branch

Kathiann M. Kowalski

Lerner Publications Company
Minneapolis

Lerner Publications Company
A division of Lerner Publishing Group, Inc.
241 First Avenue North
Minneapolis, MN 55401 U.S.A.

Website address: www.lernerbooks.com

Library of Congress Cataloging-in-Publication Data

Kowalski, Kathiann M., 1955–
    Judges and courts: a look at the judicial branch / By Kathiann M. Kowalski.
        p.   cm. — (Searchlight books™—how does government work?)
    Includes index.
    ISBN 978–0–7613–6516–7 (lib. bdg. : alk. paper)
    1. Courts—United States—Juvenile literature. 2. Procedure (Law)—United States—Juvenile literature. 3. Law—United States—Juvenile literature. I. Title.
KF8720.K69 2012
347.73'1—dc22   2010041795

Manufactured in the United States of America
1 – DP – 12/31/11

Contents

Chapter 1

REAL-LIFE COURT CASES

Real-life court cases aren't quite like the ones on TV. They don't follow a script. They don't end in an hour. But they are dramatic. And they affect real people. They can even affect kids!

This is a scene from the TV show *Law & Order: Los Angeles*. How are real-life court cases different from the ones on TV?

Consider this case. A fourth-grade boy wears a T-shirt to school with the name of his favorite sports team printed on it. His school bans clothing printed with messages. His teacher makes him turn his shirt inside out. The boy thinks it's unfair. His parents agree. They take the case to court.

Courts handle cases like this every day. The cases affect real-life people—people just like you.

Sometimes kids are involved in court cases. Courts are used to settle disagreements between people or between a person and the government.

Who's Who?

Like any drama, courts have a cast of characters. The plaintiff is the person who goes to court for help. The defendant is the person accused of doing something wrong. Lawyers argue each side of the case. They ask witnesses questions. Witnesses have special knowledge of the case. A group of people called a jury listens to the case. They decide if the defendant is guilty.

Sometimes plaintiffs and defendants accept a jury's decision. Other times, they appeal. This means they go to another court to try to get the decision changed.

This picture shows a lawyer (LEFT) asking a witness (RIGHT) questions in front of a judge (CENTER). A judge's job is to know the law and to keep the court in order.

Where the Courts Fit In

The courts have a big job. But they don't work alone. Where do they fit into the government? The answer is in the U.S. Constitution. The Constitution guarantees rights for all Americans. These rights appear in amendments (changes people made throughout the years) within the Constitution. The Constitution also sets up a federal (national) system of government.

Within the federal system, three parts share the government's work. The parts are called branches. The three branches are the legislative branch, the executive branch, and the judicial branch.

This is the first page of the U.S. Constitution. The entire Constitution is four pages.

Congress is the legislative branch. It is made up of the Senate and the House of Representatives. The legislative branch makes laws.

The executive branch enforces laws. The president leads the executive branch.

PRESIDENT BARACK OBAMA
SPEAKS TO THE SENATE AND THE
HOUSE OF REPRESENTATIVES.

The courts make up the judicial branch. When disagreements about the law come up, the judicial branch interprets the laws. In other words, it decides what laws mean. It decides things like whether free-speech laws mean a student has the right to wear a T-shirt with the name of a sports team printed on it.

Judges have to know the law well. This knowledge helps them run their courtrooms and decide cases.

JUDGE STEV

What Is the Law?

You know the judicial branch interprets the law. But what are laws?

Laws are rules made by the government. Statutes are laws that are written down. Criminal statutes say people can't harm others. Those who disobey criminal statutes may go to jail.

When someone breaks a criminal statute, a police officer arrests him or her.

Civil statutes have to do with business, health, and other subjects. Those who disobey civil statutes might have to pay back money lost because of their actions. For example, let's say a baker and a grocer agree that the baker will supply baked goods to the grocer. If the baker breaks the agreement, the baker may have to pay the grocer money lost because of the broken agreement.

Unlike statutes, common laws aren't written anywhere. Common law is "judge-made law." Common laws develop when judges make decisions in certain court cases. When similar cases arise later, judges look at earlier decisions. They try to treat similar cases the same way.

When a baker makes a written agreement with someone to provide bread, he is entering a legal agreement. If he breaks that agreement, the other person can take him to court.

Chapter 2

COURTS FROM TOP TO BOTTOM

The United States has two court systems, the state system and the federal system. State courts handle issues that affect states. Federal courts deal with matters that affect the whole country.

The federal court system is independent from the executive and legislative branches. The independence helps courts make fair decisions. Courts aren't pressured by the other branches.

The Hawaii Supreme Court is part of the state court system. What is the other court system in the United States?

A Balancing Act

The country's founders didn't want any one branch to have all the power. The Constitution sets up checks and balances to limit federal courts' power. Checks and balances are ways each branch keeps the others from getting too powerful.

Impeachment is one example of a check and balance. *Impeach* means "to accuse of wrongdoing." The House of Representatives can impeach a judge if the judge does something very wrong. When a judge is impeached, the Senate holds a trial. If two-thirds of the Senate agrees the judge did something wrong, the judge loses his or her job.

Some members of Congress pose in front of the U.S. Capitol. Congress checks the power of the judicial branch by being able to impeach judges who do something wrong.

A Pyramid

The federal court system is like a pyramid. The Supreme Court is on top. Its nine judges form the country's highest court.

Thirteen courts of appeal sit below the Supreme Court. Courts of appeal are courts where plaintiffs and defendants can take their cases to try to have juries' decisions changed.

The nine Supreme Court judges pose for a photo in 2010. They are (FROM LEFT) Clarence Thomas, Sonia Sotomayor, Antonin Scalia, Stephen Breyer, John Roberts, Samuel Alito, Anthony Kennedy, Elena Kagan, and Ruth Bader Ginsburg.

This federal district courthouse is in Brooklyn, New York.

Beneath the courts of appeal are federal district courts. These are general trial courts. Each district covers a geographic area. Every state, plus the District of Columbia and Puerto Rico, has at least one federal district.

Each federal district also has a bankruptcy court. These courts deal with people and companies that can't pay their debts.

State Courts

Each state has its own court system. Most state court systems have a pyramid structure, just like the federal courts. The highest court in each state system has the last word on state law. An example of such a court is the New York State Court of Appeals.

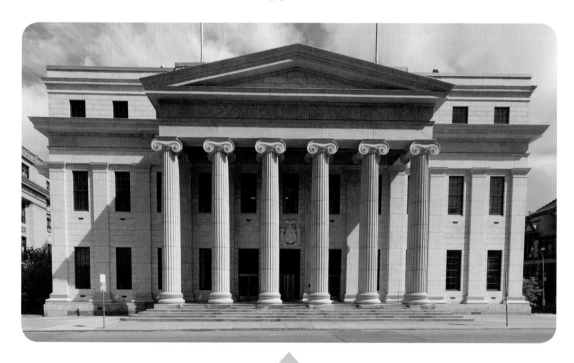

THE NEW YORK STATE COURT OF APPEALS HAS THE FINAL SAY IN CASES THAT INVOLVE NEW YORK STATE LAW.

Cases start in a general trial court like this one in Arizona.

A state's general trial courts form the bottom layer. They usually try both civil and criminal cases.

Most states have appeals courts between the state's highest court and the general trial courts. These courts hear appeals from the trial courts. States with small populations may let appeals go straight to the state's highest court.

Chapter 3

THE SUPREME COURT

"I'll take this case to the Supreme Court!" People say this when they feel strongly about a case. But getting a case to the Supreme Court is hard.

Throughout the year, Supreme Court judges consider requests for the Court to hear a case. If four out of nine judges vote to hear a case, the Court will do so.

The Supreme Court Building is in Washington, D.C. How many Supreme Court judges must vote to hear a case before it goes to the Supreme Court?

Deciding Cases

Once the Supreme Court decides to hear a case, both sides' lawyers send papers called briefs to the Court. Briefs discuss each side's arguments. Then the lawyers go to Court to argue their case.

Later in the week, the judges meet to discuss the case. Then they vote. For a case to win, more than half of the Court's judges have to vote in favor of it.

This man is holding a copy of the brief filed with the U.S. Supreme Court on his behalf. The opposing side also filed a brief.

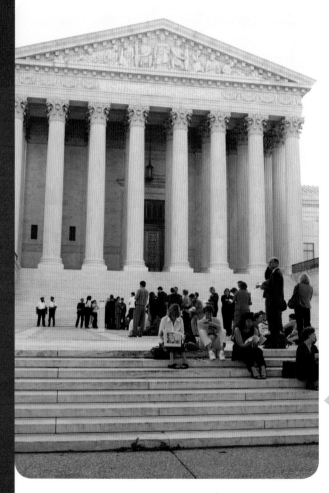

Often the Court publishes a written opinion about its decision. A member of the winning side writes the opinion. All the judges read the opinion. After the opinions have been read, the Court finally announces its decision.

THIS GROUP IS WAITING OUTSIDE FOR THE SUPREME COURT TO ANNOUNCE ITS DECISION IN A CASE.

Chapter 4

CRIMINAL LAW

The Constitution gives everyone the right to a lawyer. The country's founders felt all people deserved a fair trial. The courts treat criminal defendants as innocent until they are proven guilty.

This painting shows the founders signing the Constitution. What is one right that the Constitution gives us?

What Is a Crime?

A crime is an act that harms people or communities. Felonies are the most serious crimes. Robbery is a felony. Less serious crimes, such as littering, are called misdemeanors.

Under our Constitution, laws must clearly say what actions are considered crimes. Unclear laws are unconstitutional.

Littering is a misdemeanor. Most people who commit misdemeanors are punished with a fine. Felonies often result in a prison sentence.

The Constitution also forbids ex post facto, or "after the fact," laws. The government can't decide something is a crime after people have done it and then punish them for it. Laws that single out one person or one group are unconstitutional too.

The Fifth Amendment to the Constitution says no one can "be deprived of life, liberty, or property, without due process of law." This means the government can't just lock someone up, even if police think the person committed a crime. But a person might spend time in jail during his or her trial.

The Constitution guarantees that people in the United States won't be locked up unless they have been convicted of committing a crime.

Rights and the Police

Police must respect people's rights. The Fourth Amendment forbids police from searching people or taking their things without a good reason.

Police also must read the Miranda warning when arresting someone. It lets people know that anything they say can be used against them in court. The Fifth Amendment says the government can't force people to say anything that might hurt them in court.

The Constitution provides guidelines for police when they are making arrests.

Under Arrest

Within one or two days, police must bring the defendant to court for an arraignment. That's a process where the court makes sure the defendant knows his or her rights. The court reads charges against the defendant. The defendant tells the court whether he or she pleads guilty or not guilty.

The court decides what to do about bail. Bail is money a defendant pays to stay out of jail until his or her trial. The Eighth Amendment forbids very high bail. Setting high bail would be a way of punishing someone without a trial.

A man (LEFT) and his lawyer (SECOND FROM LEFT) listen to the man's arraignment.

This picture shows an accused person and his lawyer leaving a courtroom after a pretrial hearing.

Pretrial hearings determine if the government has enough evidence for a trial. Only about 10 percent of criminal cases get to trial. Most defendants plea-bargain. Defendants who plea-bargain must plead either guilty or no contest. A no-contest plea means the defendant doesn't plead innocent or guilty. A plea-bargaining defendant loses the right to a trial. But in return, he or she gets a less severe punishment.

On Trial

The Sixth Amendment guarantees every criminal defendant a speedy and public trial. During a trial, a defendant has the right to see and hear the witnesses. A defendant also has the right to make witnesses come to court to be a part of the case.

A WITNESS ANSWERS A LAWYER'S
QUESTIONS DURING A TRIAL.

After all the evidence has been heard, lawyers make closing arguments. They explain to the jury how the evidence fits together to support their case. The judge tells the jury about the law. Then the jury meets in private. Its members talk about the case.

In general, a jury in a criminal case must give a unanimous decision. That means all jurors must agree.

This image is from the movie *Twelve Angry Men*. The movie shows a jury arguing about whether to find the defendant guilty.

Sentencing and Appeals

During sentencing, the judge says what a guilty person's punishment will be. The Eighth Amendment says punishment can't be "cruel and unusual."

About one-third of defendants who are found guilty appeal the decision. If the appeal doesn't result in a different outcome, a defendant may try more appeals. But the states' highest courts may not have to hear all appeals. And the U.S. Supreme Court chooses which cases to hear.

A judge sentences a defendant. Many states have sentencing guidelines that list fair sentences for certain crimes.

Chapter 5
CIVIL LAW

In TV shows, most court cases involve crimes such as murder. But in real life, many court cases don't involve a crime at all. They are civil cases. They involve conflicts between people or companies.

A lawyer presents evidence in a civil case. What kind of conflicts do civil cases involve?

Before the Trial

Lawsuits (legal actions) for civil cases start with a complaint. The complaint explains the reason for the lawsuit. When people have lawsuits brought against them, they are being sued. A person who is being sued must respond to the complaint or lose the case. To respond, a person can give an answer to each point in the complaint. Or he or she can make a motion. That's a formal suggestion made in court. For example, a motion to dismiss says the person who brought the complaint couldn't win even if the points in the complaint are true. This motion suggests that there is no need for a trial.

Two teams of lawyers prepare for their closing arguments in a civil case.

No Trial

Most civil cases never go to trial. Trials are costly. Often the people involved want to avoid paying lawyers. Other times, people do not want to take their chances at a trial. In most of these cases, the two sides' lawyers work out a settlement (agreement) themselves.

A group of lawyers meets to find a settlement before their case goes to trial. Most civil cases never go to trial.

Chapter 6

THE COURTS AND YOU

Young citizens say the pledge of allegiance. Why is it important for citizens to know how the courts work?

All citizens should know how the U.S. court system works. That includes you! After all, someday you might be a plaintiff or a defendant. Or you could work as a lawyer or a judge. And even if you don't become any of these things, you should still know your rights and duties as a citizen.

Jury Duty

Serving on a jury is one duty of a citizen. Jury duty is hard work. Juries must listen carefully, even if a case takes a long time or gets complicated. And they must not base decisions on personal feelings.

JURIES PICK ONE PERSON
TO READ THEIR DECISION.
THIS PERSON IS CALLED THE
PRESIDING JUROR.

People get notices in the mail telling them when they have jury duty. But not everyone who gets a notice is picked to be a juror. The judge asks potential jurors questions. Lawyers may ask questions too. Does the juror know anyone in the case? Would personal feelings keep a juror from being fair? If someone's answers suggest a problem, the court does not let that person serve on that case.

Both state and federal courts send notices for jury duty. They choose people from state lists.

Legal Careers

Working for justice is a noble goal. Maybe one day, you'll be a lawyer or even a judge. To become a lawyer, people need a college degree. Next comes law school. Finally, law students must pass a test called the bar exam.

People who become judges have usually worked as lawyers first. Depending on the court, judges may be appointed (chosen) or elected.

Law students go to classes to learn about past cases and to develop the skills to figure out legal problems.

Know Your Rights

Even if you don't choose a legal career, you should know about the U.S. court system. U.S. laws affect everyone. Read articles about court cases. Find out how the courts rule on different issues. Those court rulings could affect you.

America's court system isn't perfect. Sometimes mistakes mean that criminals go free. Sometimes results are unjust. But the court system tries hard to treat people fairly. The courts' job is to provide justice for all.

Learning what your rights are is important. You can find more information about your rights in books, on the Internet, and from your parents and teachers.

Glossary

appeal: a claim that the outcome was wrong in a court case

arraignment: a pretrial process during which the court makes sure that the defendant knows his or her rights

defendant: a person who is accused of breaking the law

evidence: information or items that tend to prove or disprove a point in a case

executive branch: the branch of government that is led by the president. The executive branch enforces the laws of the United States.

judicial branch: the branch of government involving the court system

jury: a group of people from the community who listen to a court case and decide who's innocent and who's guilty

legislative branch: the branch of government that makes laws

Miranda warning: a warning that police give when arresting someone. The Miranda warning lets people know that anything they say can be used against them in court.

plaintiff: a person who goes to court for help

plea-bargain: to plead guilty or no contest in exchange for a less severe punishment

sentence: to say what a guilty person's punishment will be

settlement: an agreement among the people in a case. Cases that are settled do not go to trial.

trial: the formal procedure in which a court hears evidence and decides the outcome of a case

witness: a person with special knowledge of a court case

Learn More about Government

Books

DiPrimio, Pete. *The Judicial Branch*. Hockessin, DE: Mitchell Lane, 2011. Find out all about the judicial branch in this selection.

Gorman, Jacqueline Laks. *Why Do We Have Laws?* Pleasantville, NY: Weekly Reader Books, 2008. Read about laws and why we have them.

McElroy, Lisa Tucker. *Sonia Sotomayor: First Hispanic U.S. Supreme Court Justice*. Minneapolis: Lerner Publications Company, 2010. Check out this in-depth biography of Sonia Sotomayor, the first Hispanic American to become a Supreme Court judge.

Taylor-Butler, Christine. *The Supreme Court*. New York: Children's Press, 2008. Read more about the nation's highest court in this interesting book.

Websites

Ben's Guide to U.S. Government for Kids
http://bensguide.gpo.gov/3-5/index.html
This useful website is full of information about the U.S. government and how it works.

Time for Kids: A Look at the Supreme Court
http://www.timeforkids.com/TFK/specials/
articles/0,6709,1103946,00.html
At this site, you can meet the Supreme Court judges, get answers to questions about the court, and learn about historic Supreme Court cases.

United States Government for Kids
http://library.thinkquest.org/5873
Visit this page designed by students to read all about the government, its branches, and more.

Index

Photo Acknowledgments

The images in this book are used with the permission of: AP Photo/Chris Haston/NBC/NBCU Photo Bank, p. 4; © Laura Dwight/Stock Connection Distribution/Alamy, p. 5; © iStockphoto.com/Rich Legg, p. 6; National Archives, p. 7; © Scott J. Ferrell/CQ-Roll Call Group/Getty Images, p. 8; © Peter Dazeley/Photographer's Choice RF/Getty Images, p. 9; © Jack Dagley Photography/Shutterstock.com, p. 10; © iStockphoto.com/ Rudyanto Wijaya, p. 11; © David L. Moore - Oahu/Alamy, p. 12; © Mark Wilson/Getty Images, p. 13; © Chip Somodevilla/Getty Images, p. 14; © Peter Bennett/Ambient Images/Photolibrary, p. 15; © Matt H. Wade/ CC-BY-SA-3.0/Wikipedia, p. 16; AP Photo/Matt York, p. 17; © Royalty-Free/CORBIS, pp. 18, 23; AP Photo/ Gerald Herbert, p. 19; © Douglas Graham/CQ-Roll Call Group/Getty Images, p. 20; Library of Congress LC-USZC4-2541, p. 21; © JHDT Stock Images LLC/Shutterstock.com, p. 22; © Bill Fritsch/Brand X Pictures/ Getty Images, p. 24; © Mike Albans/NY Daily News Archive/Getty Images, p. 25; REUTERS/Rebecca Cook, p. 26; © Image Source/Getty Images, p. 27; Everett Collection, p. 28; © Rich Legg/Vetta/Getty Images, p. 29; © rubberball/Getty Images, p. 30; AP Photo/Journal Times, Mark Hertzberg, p. 31; © Tim Klein/The Image Bank/Getty Images, p. 32; © Comstock Images, pp. 33, 37; © moodboard/the Agency Collection/ Getty Images, p. 34; © Comstock Images/Getty Images, p. 35; © Ricky Carioti/The Washington Post/Getty Images, p. 36.

Front cover: © Chip Somodevilla/Getty Images.

Main body text set in Adrianna Regular 14/20.
Typeface provided by Chank.